EVERYDAY GUIDES
MADE EASY

SAMSUNG
ANDROID
BASICS

This is a **FLAME TREE** book
First published 2015

Publisher and Creative Director: Nick Wells
Project Editor: Laura Bulbeck
Art Director: Mike Spender
Layout Design: Jane Ashley
Digital Design and Production: Chris Herbert
Copy Editor: Daniela Nava
Screenshots: Michael Sawh
Proofreader: Wendy Hobson
Indexer: Helen Snaith

Special thanks to: Polly Prior, Frances Bodiam and Helen Crust

This edition first published 2015 by
FLAME TREE PUBLISHING
Crabtree Hall, Crabtree Lane
Fulham, London SW6 6TY
United Kingdom

www.flametreepublishing.com

15 17 19 18 16
1 3 5 7 9 10 8 6 4 2

ISBN 978-1-78361-391-5

A CIP record for this book is available from the British Library
upon request.

Printed in China

EVERYDAY GUIDES
MADE EASY

SAMSUNG ANDROID BASICS

MICHAEL SAWH

SERIES FOREWORD BY MARK MAYNE

FLAME TREE
PUBLISHING

CONTENTS

Get started with a detailed guide through the process of
setting up your phone or tablet for the very first time.

Navigate your way around your device and perform
basic functions like calls, texts and customization.

These step-by-step guides will have you surfing the net,
emailing and using maps in no time.

Find out which apps come pre-installed and how to
find and download new ones.

Find out how to use your Samsung Android device as a camera,
video recorder and music player.

SERIES FOREWORD

Since Apple launched the iPhone in 2007 and followed it up with the iPad, the consumer touchscreen technology sector has increased exponentially. There is now a bewildering variety of choices to make about the smartphone and tablet devices we carry with us, but this *Samsung Android Basics* guide is here to help you navigate many of them.

Whether you're looking for entertainment, music, social connectivity, any business service you can think of, or a source of information about where you are and what you're looking at that very second, this *Samsung Android Basics* guide will help you navigate the world of touchscreen tech and apps.

In this series we take a detailed look at the device, how to set it up and get the best out of it for your lifestyle, as well as how to get to grips with the basics of the operating system. Don't worry, though – this guide is designed for absolute beginners, as well as those who are looking for more expert knowledge.

Finally there's a comprehensive troubleshooting guide, full of the best tips and tricks to keep you and your device working in perfect harmony. Throughout each chapter there are Hot Tips to save you time and effort – keep a sharp eye out!

This easy-to-use, step-by-step guide is written by a recognized expert in their field, so you can be sure of the best advice and the latest knowledge without breaking a sweat. The *Samsung Android Basics* guide is an asset to any reference bookshelf – happy reading.

Mark Mayne
Editor of T3.com

INTRODUCTION

The great thing about owning a tablet or a smartphone is that they can do many of the things your desktop computer or laptop can do, whether that's browsing the internet, sending emails, watching video or even playing games. Best of all, they can do it all in a smaller, more bag or pocket-friendly design so you can carry it around wherever you go. Android is the operating system that Samsung (and various other) mobile devices use, and this book is here to give helpful hints and clear advice on how to go about using it.

STEP-BY-STEP GUIDES

Using a tablet or smartphone can be daunting at first, but they are actually designed to be very easy to use. In the following five chapters we will provide you with the key information plus some handy tips to help you quickly get to grips with your new Samsung Android phone or tablet from the very first time you push the power button, as well as tackle some of those trickier features. Many of the explanations are broken down into step-by-step instructions, which are easy to follow.

Above: Step-by-step instructions will guide you through various processes, including setting up for the first time.

HOT TIPS

Throughout the book you will find little yellow boxes called 'Hot Tips' giving brief handy hints and extra pieces of advice.

DIFFERENT VERSIONS

Before you read on, it's important to know that not all Samsung Android phones and tablets are the same. That's because they can include different features and, more importantly, run on different versions of Android. This is the software that your device uses to create the place you can explore when you press that power button.

Some older Samsung Android tablets and smartphones will run on Android Ice Cream Sandwich 4.0, with newer models using either Android 4.1 Jelly Bean or Android 4.4 KitKat. What this means is that some devices might not be able to access some of the features mentioned in this book. We will do our best to mention, where possible, those features that will only work on newer devices, to help explain why you are missing out.

Above: The Galaxy Alpha (left) runs on Android 4.4 Kitkat, whilst the Galaxy Core (right) runs on Android 4.1 Jelly Bean.

GETTING STARTED

INTRODUCTION TO SAMSUNG ANDROID

Samsung smartphones and tablets are popular devices, and they run Android software that lets users call, text, customize, browse the internet, email, play music, take photos and so much more.

WHAT IS ANDROID?

Android is an operating system created by Google and it runs on a growing number of smartphones and tablets. Just like the iOS operating system that runs on iPhones, Android is based around a set of home screens; you can use your touchscreen display to access apps, browse the internet, play games and much more.

The key difference between Apple's iOS and Google's Android is that you have more freedom to customize how the latter looks.

Android lets you do many things that you can also do with Google on a computer, such as searching for information, watching videos and answering emails – and that's just the beginning.

Above: Android allows for much more customization than iOS.

WHAT IS TOUCHWIZ?

Samsung puts its own twist on Android with TouchWiz, which is a user interface that lies on top of Android. You can still do all the things you'd expect Android phones and tablets to offer, plus there are some extra features that are unique to Samsung devices.

The reason why Samsung uses TouchWiz is to help you make better use of some of the unique features that you can only find on Samsung Android devices.

Samsung and TouchWiz combined can be presented slightly differently on older tablets and smartphones. However, the core features are largely the same so you won't miss out on anything that later devices, such as the Samsung Galaxy Tab and Galaxy S5, enjoy.

Above: TouchWiz is Samsung's unique take on Android.

SETTING UP YOUR DEVICE

Now that you have taken your new Samsung Android device out of its packaging, these are the essential steps you need to go through in order to get it ready for proper use.

Hot Tip

Before switching on for the first time, charge the device with the supplied charger to make sure that there is enough power to complete the setup process.

GETTING READY FOR SETUP

First, make sure that the battery and SIM card are in place. The SIM card is the small piece of plastic that holds a chip and carries all of the data, enabling you to make calls and access the internet. Newer phone handsets, such as the Samsung Galaxy S5, use the smaller nano SIM cards, which should be supplied when purchasing the phone brand new. SIM cards usually fit in a compartment alongside the battery, behind the removable back cover of the phone. For tablets, the SIM card slot can usually be found hidden behind a small latch on the top or the side of the device.

LANGUAGE AND COUNTRY

Now, switch on your phone. Once the Samsung logo has disappeared, you will need to select your language and country. Android will choose the most likely option, known as the default. If you want to change this to something else, tap on the small arrow in the corner of the Select language box, then swipe down to find the right country and press to replace.

Above: Select the correct language.

Above: Accessibility can be adjusted after the setup process is completed; if you prefer.

Above: You will find many more accessibility options under Settings.

ACCESSIBILITY (OPTIONAL)

If you suffer from any visual or hearing impairment, Samsung offers a range of settings which help to make the device easier to use. Press Settings then Accessibility to display the options available, which are broken down into sections for vision, hearing, and dexterity and interaction. These can be adjusted now or later, once you have finished the setup process.

ACCESSIBILITY FEATURES

There are many ways to make your Samsung device easier to use. Scroll through the list to see the options; here are some core accessibility features you should look out for.

- **Talkback:** This enables the phone or tablet to read out what's on the screen. Press the Talkback button to turn the option on or off. It can also be used to help you get in position when the camera is turned on.

- **Font Size:** If you need to make the text on menu screens or web pages easier to see, you can select from a range of more reader-friendly font sizes.

- **Magnification Gestures:** Turning this mode on will let you zoom in and out of pages by triple-tapping the screen.

- **Accessibility Shortcut:** This will give you quicker access to accessibility options. When turned on, you can press the power key and wait until you hear a sound or feel the phone or tablet vibrate. Alternatively, you can tap and hold the power key until there's audio confirmation that the shortcut is enabled.

- **Text-to-speech Options:** Whatever you type into the phone or tablet will be

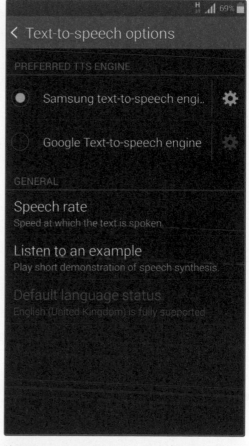

Above: Turn on Text-to-speech Options to turn what you type into audio.

translated into audio feedback. There is both Samsung text-to-speech, which will read aloud information within Samsung's own applications and Google text-to-speech, for Google's apps.

○ **Mono Audio**: A feature for those suffering from hearing difficulties, this can set the sound from stereo to mono when you are using just one earphone.

CONNECT TO A WIRELESS NETWORK

This is one of the most important parts of the setup and is necessary in order to continue any further. You can use a mobile internet connection, but it's recommended that you use a secure Wi-Fi connection. This means setting up your device at home is probably the best option.

1. Swipe the **Wi-Fi toggle** to begin scanning for available internet connections.

2. A list of **available Wi-Fi networks** should now be displayed. If the one you were hoping would appear is not shown, a button below the list of connections will let you scan for other Wi-Fi networks.

3. Once the correct Wi-Fi network is detected, this should have a **padlock** icon beside it. Press it and you will be prompted to type in the password, which can usually

Step 2: Select the Wi-Fi network you want or scan for others.

Hot Tip

'Advanced options', which can be found by pressing the three dots in the top right corner, can provide additional details on the Wi-Fi connection, including signal strength.

be found somewhere on the router. This also brings up the on-screen keyboard where you can type in the password.

4. You can choose to **show the password** as you type it in but it's safer to keep this concealed.

5. Once the password is typed in, press Connect. If you are successful, the connection should state whether you are connected or not. Press Next down in the bottom right-hand corner to proceed.

Step 5: A tick or the word Connected will signify when you are successfully connected to a Wi-Fi network.

EULA AGREEMENT

You'll need to agree to the terms of the licence that comes when buying a Samsung device. This includes user rights on accessing the software, and agreeing that Samsung will use some of your data to improve product support and be able to make updates to software. When you've read through the text and agreed, press on the box next to the statement 'I understand and agree to the terms and conditions'.

DIAGNOSTIC AND USAGE DATA AGREEMENT (OPTIONAL)

Samsung offers to collect diagnostic and usage data to help improve its services. This could be information based on how you use applications, or log information on errors or unexpected shutdowns. You can select 'Yes' to opt in or 'No' if you don't want to take part. Select Next to continue.

GOOGLE ACCOUNT

You will then be asked whether you have a Google account. You need this to access the core software and features available on all Android devices.

Hot Tip

Improve accuracy in pinpointing your current location by choosing High Accuracy to use GPS, Wi-Fi and mobile data. This can be turned on in the Location settings.

EULA & Diagnostic Data

End User Licence Agreement for Software

IMPORTANT. READ CAREFULLY: This End User Licence Agreement ("EULA") is a legal agreement between you (either an individual or a single entity) and

I understand and agree to the terms and conditions above.

CONSENT TO PROVIDE DIAGNOSTIC AND USAGE DATA

Samsung would like your help in improving the quality and performance of its products and services. Samsung and its affiliates may collect diagnostic

Yes

No thanks

Next

Above: Read thoroughly before accepting the terms.

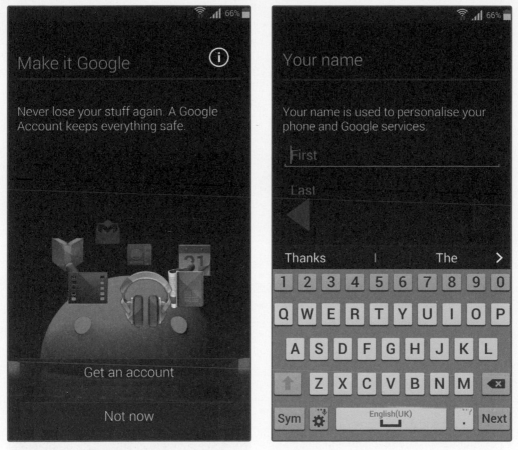

Above: A Google account will give you access to a host of useful features.

Above: Use the on-screen keyboard to type in the relevant information.

Create a Google Account

If you already have a Google account, you can simply log in using your Gmail address and password.

If you don't already have a Google account, select No and you'll be given the option to Get an account. Then take the following simple steps to create a Google account for the first time.

1. Type in your **first and last name** to personalize the account. The on-screen virtual keyboard will appear below to let you type this information in. Once finished, select the **Done** key on the keyboard.

2. Next you'll need to set up a **Gmail account** as part of your Google account. This will be used to receive email updates about Google services, and can also be used as a normal email account. Type in an email address name.

3. Create a **password** and retype it to confirm it. Use something that's memorable but not so obvious that someone could easily decipher it.

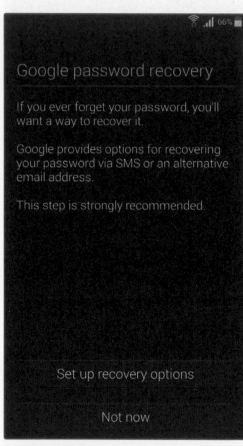

4. Don't use a password that you have already used somewhere else. Try to use a **mixture** of numbers and letters.

5. As you type, the device will indicate whether you have a **weak or strong** password.

6. Hit **Done** on the keyboard and proceed.

Google Password Recovery

If you ever forget your password, this is a really good way for you to recover it, as it can be sent to you via SMS text message or an alternative email address. This step, therefore, is highly recommended.

Above: Press Set up recovery options; or press Not now to set up the recovery options later in the phone's Settings menu.

1. Press **Set up recovery options**. Here you can input your phone number, which might have been pulled through already if the SIM card has already been recognized. You can also type in a secondary email address and the country you reside in.

2. Hit **Done** on the keyboard and then press the arrow on the right to proceed to the next part of the setup process.

Turning on Google Services

Here is where you can decide where your data on the Samsung Android device is stored and used to improve key services and features.

Backup and Restore

Tick the box to agree for data, including apps, app settings, system settings and Wi-Fi passwords, to be backed up to your Google account.

Location

Here you can turn on location data, which can be used for apps such as map navigation and helps to determine your current position. It's important to remember that turning this on can have an impact on battery life, and you can choose whether to turn it on and off outside of the setup process (in Settings).

Communication

Tick the box to opt in to be kept up to date with news and offers from Google Play. This

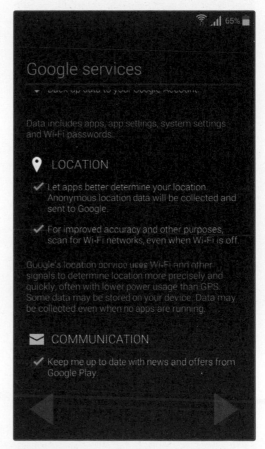

Above: Choose how much data can be used to improve Google settings.

Above: Location data (*see* page 21) is useful for such apps as maps.

Above: Select which language you would like to read the Google terms of service in.

is the storefront where you can download apps, movies, books, games and music. If you prefer not to be littered with more emails, pick **No**.

Complete Google Account

Lastly, you need to agree to Google Terms of Service and privacy policy, Chrome Terms of Service and privacy notice, and Google Play Terms of Service.

1. If you want to read them, each of the items can be **clicked to expand**. This will let you select the language before proceeding to read the various sections.

2. Once you are satisfied, you can **accept** and **agree** to make the account or **opt not to** create the account.

3. If you do the latter, you can still set up the device by moving to a new screen, which will prompt you to create a **Samsung account** instead.

4. If you accept, the device will connect to Google over the network connection to **authenticate** it. This process could take as long as five minutes to complete.

GOOGLE+ ACCOUNT (OPTIONAL)

Google+ is a social network just like Facebook or Twitter. Apart from sharing posts with other Google+ users, it's a place where you can automatically back up photos, make videos calls and send messages. Again, it is not vital to sign up at this stage and the process can be completed later (*see* page 97).

Hot Tip

Google+ is Google's social networking site where you can also automatically back up all your photos to the Cloud.

🛜 📶 64% 🔋

Upgrade to Google+

 A stream of stuff that you're into
Connect with close friends and explore common interests.

 Automatic photo backup
Back up photos as you take them, with free and private storage.

 Video calling & messaging
Enjoy texting, photos and free group video calls with Hangouts.

Get started

Not now

Above: You can set up a Google+ account after the setup is complete, if you prefer.

Create a Google+ Account

Create a profile by typing in your name and selecting your gender.

Creating a public profile where private data will be on show means that you will need to agree to Google's terms of service regarding the sharing of this information. If you are not sure, keep it private.

GOOGLE PLAY

Like the iTunes Store for Apple, this is a dedicated store where you can download Android apps, games, books, films and more. Much of this content is free but there are also things that you can buy. Assigning a Google account during the setup process, sets up the Google Play account as well.

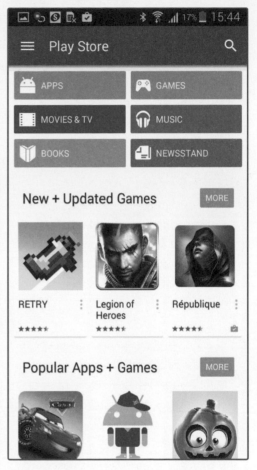

Above: Set up your credit card to make instant purchases through Google Play.

Above: Google Play provides access to a multitude of apps, music, games and more.

Add a Credit Card for Google Play Purchases

You can now set up a credit card synced to your Google Play account in order to purchase content more quickly. Alternatively, you can also create your account after you've finished the setup process (*see* page 89).

SAMSUNG ACCOUNT

Having a Samsung account, much like a Google account, will give you access to additional content, like apps, and activate modes such as Find My Mobile. This is similar to Apple's Find my Phone, which will help you to track and control your phone remotely if it goes missing.

Create a Samsung Account

1. You can **sign in** if you already have an existing Samsung account, create an account or sign in with your Google ID. Your Google ID is assigned to the email address that you used to set up your Google account earlier.

2. Alternatively, you also have the option to use your **Facebook login** information to sign in. Press the Facebook button to open up the site's web page where you can sign in and sync the accounts together.

3. Type in your **email ID** and a **password**, along with selecting your date of birth.

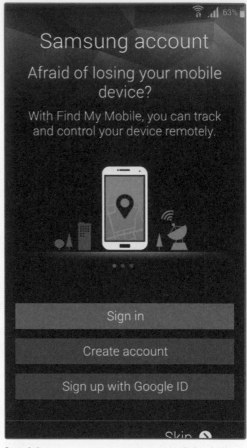

Step 1: Sign in to an existing account, sign in with Google ID or create a new account.

4. There is the option to choose whether you want to receive **marketing information**. If you don't, press the box beside it to deselect it.

5. You'll need to accept the **terms and conditions**, including how your information is handled and something called the data combination policy. Press the boxes to tick

them when you are happy with what you have read and then press the **Agree** button to proceed.

6. The last step is to **verify the account** by opening the email account you registered. This can be done after the full setup process is completed.

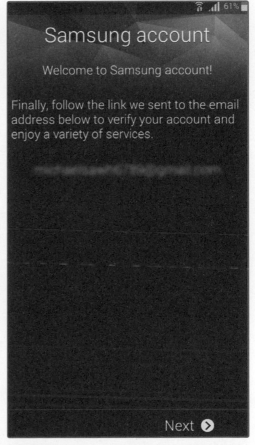

Step 2: You can also use your Facebook login details to create a Samsung account.

Step 6: Verify your account by clicking the link sent to your email address.

DROPBOX

Most Samsung phones and tablets now offer Dropbox storage. This is an application that can automatically save photos and videos to Dropbox servers you can access through a computer, your phone or tablet any time you are online. Therefore, if you lose the phone, you won't lose of all your content. If you already have an account, you can sign in with those login details, or you can set up a new account by entering your first and last name, a different email and password.

SETUP COMPLETE

You are almost done! You can now view or edit the device name, in order to make it more identifiable when using Bluetooth, Wi-Fi or tethering – but more about this later.

Above: Dropbox gives you more storage for documents, video and pictures.

Hot Tip

Setting up a Samsung account will give you exclusive access to apps and offers on services and software.

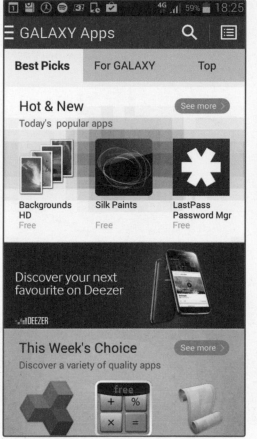

Above: By setting up a Samsung account you now have access to Galaxy Apps.

Above: Select the box to enable Easy Mode, which will simplify the home screen layout.

EASY MODE

Some Android phones also offer the option to enable an Easy mode. This essentially simplifies the home screen layout by making text and icons larger. Clicking the 'Learn more' text will give you more details about the feature, and simply selecting the box to enable Easy mode will set it up for you before leaving the setup process. Press **Finish** and you are ready to explore your device.

USING YOUR DEVICE

GETTING TO KNOW YOUR DEVICE

You've made it through the setup, so now it's time to get to know the key features of your Samsung Android phone or tablet.

HOME SCREEN

This is the place where you will spend the most time. There are multiple home screens and if you want to move to a new one, then swipe right or left across the screen. The white dots and, on later models, the icon shaped like a house will indicate which home screen you are currently viewing.

Add Home Screens

If you would like extra home screens, just follow these simple steps to adding more:

1. **Press and hold** down on anywhere on the screen.

2. **Swipe left** on the screen until you reach a screen with a + sign.

3. **Press the** + to add another home screen where you can display apps and folders.

Remove Home Screens

1. If you would prefer fewer home screens, place **two fingers** on the screen and **pinch** them together.

2. You will now be able to **swipe left** and right through all of the currently present home screens.

3. To remove one, press down on the one you no longer want and **drag** it to the **dustbin icon**.

Move App Icons

When you start up your Samsung phone or tablet for the first time, you will find that some apps are already present on the home screen. This means that they are already installed on the device. In order to drag an app icon to another home screen, press down with a finger on the icon and drag it left or right to another home screen.

Above: Drag to the dustbin icon to delete.

Delete App Icons

You can also remove an icon from the home screen by pressing and dragging it up to the dustbin icon. This won't entirely delete or uninstall the app from the phone or tablet, though.

Dock

At the bottom of the screen is a line of apps. These offer a shortcut to the most commonly used apps, such as contacts, messages, and the internet browser.

Wallpapers

Another way to personalize the home screen is to change the wallpaper, which can be static or dynamic, i.e. animated. To change the wallpaper:

1. **Press down** on the screen with a finger.

2. Select **Wallpapers** and select to change the wallpaper on the home screen.

3. You will have a **series of options** to choose from; swipe to scroll through them.

4. Once you have found the one you want, press **Set wallpaper**; when you return to the home screen, it will be updated with the new look.

Widgets

A widget is another way to customize home screens. It's a shortcut for apps and can display useful information in real time. Samsung Android phones and tablets come with a set of built-in widgets, such as a clock, a weather widget and an alarm. Android devices running on Android 4.0 Ice Cream Sandwich or above can also re-size widgets. Many Android apps also support widgets that you can add to your home screens.

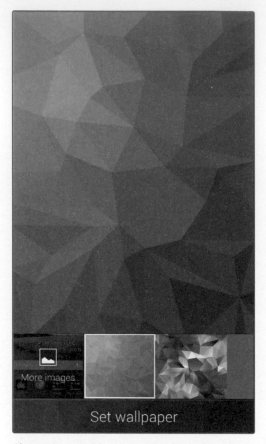

Above: Take your pick from animated and static wallpapers.

Hot Tip

You can use your own photos and images as wallpaper on newer devices by selecting 'More images' when you want to set a new wallpaper.

Above: Widgets come in different shapes and sizes.

1. Press down anywhere on the home screen with your finger and select the **Widgets** option.

2. Find the widget you want to add, then **press and hold** it.

3. You can now **drag it** to any home screen.

4. If you need to **remove** a widget, press down on it and drag it to the **dustbin icon**.

App Drawer

A key Android feature is the app drawer. This is a place where all of your apps live, away from the home screen. It can be launched via the app drawer icon at the bottom of the home screen, and you'll be able to view all your apps in a custom or alphabetical order.

App Folders

Another way to organize apps is to group them together in folders, which appear on the home screen. This is a feature that will work on devices running on Android Jelly Bean 4 and above.

1. Press and hold down on an app, and choose **Create folder**.

2. Name the folder using the pop up keyboard and then **hit the +** to begin adding apps from the app drawer by checking the boxes alongside them.

3. The new folder will appear in the **app drawer**. In order to move it to a **home screen**, press and hold the icon then drag it on to the home screen.

4. Once on the home screen, you can **drag** apps and **drop** them into the folder.

Above: The app drawer launcher can be found at the bottom of the main home screen.

Hot Tip

You can alphabetize your apps. In the app drawer, select the option for View Type. Now you are able to reorganize.

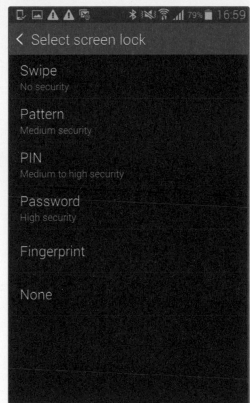

LOCK SCREEN

This prevents the screen from being activated by accident when it's in your pocket or bag.

Select Type of Lock Screen Security

This is available on Android 4.1 Jelly Bean and above.

Step 3: Choose the type of screen lock. The Samsung Galaxy S5, for example, can use a fingerprint sensor to secure the lock screen.

1. Go to **Settings** and select **Lock screen**. (Or in Kitkat, go to Settings, then Security, then Lock screen).

2. Under Screen Security press **Screen lock**.

3. You can now choose whether you want to use a **Swipe**, **Pattern**, **PIN** or **Password** to unlock Lock screen.

4. Once you have selected the type of **screen security** you want, it will be applied the next time you turn on the phone or tablet.

Above: Internet signal, battery strength and the time can all be seen at the top of the device.

Above: Status indicators will always appear along the top of your phone or tablet, no matter what menu you are on.

STATUS INDICATORS

- **Smart Stay**: This is a feature unique to Samsung which uses eye-tracking technology to detect when you are looking at the screen and turns the display to sleep when you are not.

- **Time**: The current time is one of the permanent notifications that permanently appear on the notification bar.

- **Battery Status**: This is a visual indication of how much battery life is left; the percentage beside it gives you a more precise reading. When you get below 20 per cent, the device will flash up a message to suggest plugging into the power adapter.

- **Signal Strength**: The more bars you see, the better the signal for making calls and sending text messages.

- **Internet Strength**: When you are connected to a Wi-Fi connection, the fan icon will appear, and the more lit up this is, the stronger the connection. When you are using a mobile internet connection, this will often be displayed by a small 3G or 4G or H+ icon in the status bar at the top of the device.

NOTIFICATIONS

Notifications are like small alerts, telling you when you have received information on your device, such as a missed call or even an update on Facebook. These notifications appear as small icons at the top of the screen.

Above: You can access notifications from any home screen.

Notification Bar

At the very top of the screen you will usually find a series of icons – although on some older devices they will appear at the bottom. Some will appear all the time and are the status indicators. Others, on the other hand, relate to running apps and software.

Hot Tip

In order to get rid of all of the notifications at once, press Clear and they will all disappear.

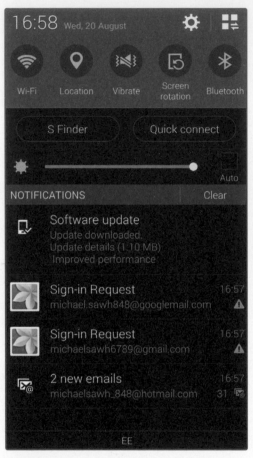

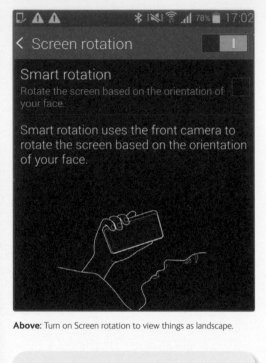

Above: Turn on Screen rotation to view things as landscape.

Above: Open the notification tray to see a list of active notifications.

Hot Tip

Turn on Screen rotation in Settings when you need to view a video or picture in landscape mode.

Notification Tray

There is another way to view notifications in greater detail, which gives you the opportunity to address them without having to launch the app.

1. Swipe down with a finger from the top of the screen, or up from the bottom of the screen if the **notification tray** lies there instead.

2. You'll see a list of **active notifications**. In order to deal with a notification, press on it and this will open the app related to it.

3. If you want to ignore the notification, **swipe right** with a finger on the notification to **dismiss** it.

Settings Toggle

As well as access to notifications, the notification tray also includes shortcuts to a series of key settings which you can quickly turn on and off by pressing on them. When they are illuminated, it means that the setting has been activated.

SETTINGS

Beyond the Quick Access Settings in the notification tray, you can also find a host of other settings by pressing the Settings cog icon. These are some of the more important ones, which will help you to customize your phone or tablet.

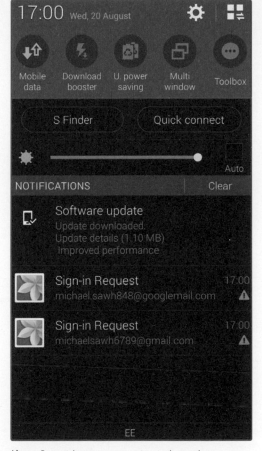

Above: Swipe right to see more settings in the toggle.

Ringtones and Notifications

If you want to change the ringtone, you can select from a range of pre-installed ones. Open Settings, select Sound and then press Ringtones. Swipe up and down to scroll through and preview the options. Once you have found the perfect one, press Add or OK to select it. To change notification sounds, when you get to the Sound screen, select Notifications instead.

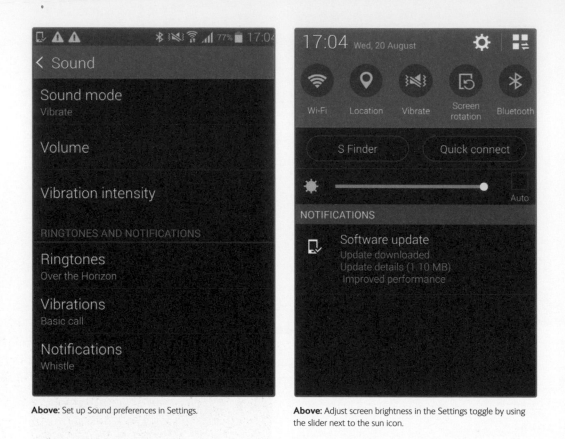

Above: Set up Sound preferences in Settings.

Above: Adjust screen brightness in the Settings toggle by using the slider next to the sun icon.

Adjusting Screen Brightness

The screen can sometimes drain a lot of power from your phone or tablet at maximum brightness, so you can turn it down to help preserve battery life. Open Settings, select Display, then Brightness. Slide to adjust screen brightness.

Alternatively, swipe down from the top of the screen (or up if you have an older Samsung Galaxy tablet) to bring up the notification tray and you'll find the small sun icon with a bar which you can swipe to brighten or darken the screen. There is also an Auto button so you can apply a default brightness level.

BASIC NAVIGATION

To use your device, there are key control features you need to understand. Main navigation will be through the touchscreen, but also through certain key buttons.

TOUCHSCREEN

The touchscreen plays a major role in the way you interact with a Samsung device, and there are two main ways of using it.

- **Swiping**: Moving your finger across the page in order to move to the next screen is a means of navigating your way around the device and will become second nature.

- **Scrolling**: If you are reading a web page, email, or a thread of text messages, or moving around an app, and wish to move up and down the page, use a finger to flick the screen up or down. The faster the flick, the quicker the page moves.

BUTTONS

There are a few buttons which Samsung Android phones and tablets will feature in order for you to use the device.

Power and Volume

All phones and tablets will have a physical on/off button and a volume rocker to quickly turn the device off or adjust the volume.

Home Button

Below the screen you will usually find one button which you can physically press and that's the home button. Pressing this once will always take you back to the main home screen. Pressing it twice in short succession will activate Samsung S Voice, which we will discuss in more detail later (*see* page 104), whereas holding it down opens Google Now.

Above: Home Button

Above: Recent Apps button (left) and Return key (Right)

Recent Apps Button

On either side of the Home button, you will find the soft keys. This is commonly found on most Samsung devices although older models include them as onscreen buttons at the bottom of the display. The one to the left, with multiple squares, is the recent apps button. This has replaced the Menu button on older models; and holding it down now brings up the menu of the app you're in.

- Pressing this once lets you see all of the **recently opened apps**.

- You can press on any of the apps to **jump back** quickly into them or you can swipe right on each of them to **dismiss** them, thus closing them. This feature works with devices running on Android 4.0 Ice Cream Sandwich or above.

- Pressing the icon with the **stack of items and a cross** will close all of the actively running apps.

- The small **pie chart icon** will show you which apps are running and how much of the power they are using.

Return Key

The soft key to the right of the home screen, which is shaped like a bent arrow, is the return key. Pressing this once will return you to the previous screen you accessed. This could be the last page in a book or a previous web page.

Above: The Recent apps button will let you see all of the currently running apps.

THE SAMSUNG KEYBOARD

Every Samsung device has a virtual onscreen keyboard that is used to type in web page URLs, text messages and pretty much anything for which you would use a normal computer keyboard. Here are some of the basics.

The Buttons

- **Arrow up**: Press this to turn the letters into capitals; hold down to keep the keyboard in capital mode.

- **Arrow with X**: This will delete a letter. Hold down to delete the entire input.

- **SYM**: This changes the keyboard to show symbols and punctuation.

- **1/2**: Press this to display the second set of symbols and punctuation.

- **Microphone**: Press this to speak the message or command.

Above: Whenever you need to type, the keyboard will appear.

Hot Tip

Turn on the Swype keyboard in the latest Samsung tablets and phones to slide your fingers across the keys and type faster. Go to Keyboard swipe in Settings and select Continuous input.

○ **Next/Go**: When you are typing a text message, the button in the bottom right corner will contain the word **Next** and when pressed will skip to the next stage of sending a message. **Go** appears when you are browsing the web and want to launch a new web page.

○ **Space**: Just like on a traditional keyboard, this adds spaces between words and characters.

Predictive Text

This will suggest words as you type on the virtual keyboard. Press on the predictive text to switch on live word update, which automatically updates with popular new words every day. It can also use the personal language data you have entered to make the prediction results better.

Auto Replace

Complete or replace the word you are typing with the most probable word when you tap the space bar or a punctuation mark.

Google Voice Typing and Search

You have the option to type just by speaking into the microphone on your Samsung Android phone and on newer Samsung Android tablets. Click the Settings cog to choose input languages, block offensive words and download languages for offline speech recognition.

Above: Predictive text will help you type faster by suggesting how you might like to finish the word.

TEXT AND PICTURE MESSAGING

SMS (text messaging) and MMS (picture messaging) are popular forms of communication. We'll show you how to get started and master the art of staying in touch.

SENDING TEXT MESSAGES

When you don't have time to speak directly to someone, you can just send them a text message. These short messages can be sent from Samsung phones, and tablets like the Galaxy Tab 3 8.0 to other phones and tablets. This can be done as long as the same SIM, micro SIM or Nano SIM card used to make phone calls is inserted in your device.

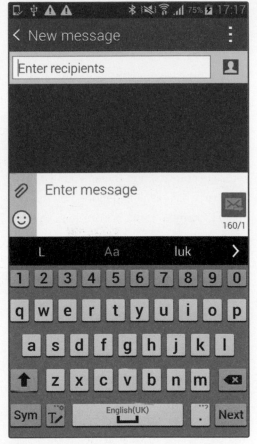

To Send a New Message

1. Locate the app icon illustrated by an **envelope** and press to launch.

2. Press the icon that looks like the **pen on a piece of paper** to open up a new message.

3. In the **Enter recipients** box, use the pop-up keyboard below to type the name of the contact you want to send

Step 3: Type the name of the person you want to send the message to in the Enter recipients box.

the message to. As you type in the letters, you should be able to see a generated list of names from your **contact list**. When you see the correct contact, press it to add it to the message.

4. In the **Enter message** field, type in your message. There's no limit on how much text you can include but longer messages will carry over into additional messages.

5. To add an **emoticon**, press the smiley face and select one.

6. Press the icon with the **envelope and arrow** to send the message when ready.

To Reply

Inside the Messages app, choose the text message conversation thread you wish to reply to, which can be identified by the sender's name or time or date sent. Open and type in the box which contains the words Enter message, then hit the send button to send your response.

Texting Multiple People

To send a text message to more than one person, follow the same steps for sending a new message and when you reach step 3, simply type in another contact and press to select and add to the existing recipients. You will be able to view all the people on the text message at the top of the screen.

Above: The number on the Messages app icon indicates the number of unread texts.

FORWARDING TEXT MESSAGES

If you want to quickly forward a text message, press and hold on the message and this will bring up a series of **Message options**. Press on **Forward** and this will open a new message with the copy pasted in below. You can now forward in the same way you send a text message.

RECEIVING TEXT MESSAGES

When the recipient of your text replies, you may see the message appear on screen. As well as this, the **Messages** app icon will include a number to indicate you have an unread message. Tap on the messages icon and you will see all the most recent text message conversations you've had.

SENDING PICTURE MESSAGES

As well as sending text messages, you can also send pictures to contacts on your phone or tablet.

1. Press **Messages** and then press the new message icon.

2. Type in the contact number of the recipient and then write the text in the **Enter message** section.

3. Press the **paperclip** to **attach** a file. You can also send notes, videos and audio clips.

4. Once you have selected the image, press the **envelope with arrow icon** to send your picture message.

Above: You can add a picture attachment to your message by pressing the paperclip.

Hot Tip

Delay message sending to give you time to cancel. Go to Settings and Messages to turn this mode on.

MAKING PHONE CALLS

Despite everything else it can now do, the core feature of a smartphone is being able to make calls. Some Samsung tablets also have call functionality and the ability to make video calls to stay in touch.

IMPORTING CONTACTS

Contacts are the numbers, email addresses and any other details that you use to communicate through your Samsung phone and specific tablets like the Samsung Galaxy Tab 7.0 Plus. Getting those contacts off an old device is not as difficult as it might first seem and here is how to do it.

Import from SIM Card

This is one of the most common ways to transfer over contracts to a new device, and this is how you do it.

Hot Tip

Samsung Kies is a PC and Mac application that you can download from the Samsung website to help import contacts via your computer.

1. Go to the **Contacts** app and press the **Settings** button.

2. Press **Contacts** and then select **Import/Export**.

3. Choose the option to **Import from SIM card**.

4. You will now see a box asking you where to save contacts; select **Device**.

5. All the contacts saved to your SIM should be viewable. Tick the box next to **Select All** and then press **Done**. The contacts will begin transferring to the phone.

IMPORTING CONTACTS FROM APPLE

Step 3: Select Import from SIM card.

If you are making the move from an iPhone or an iPad to a Samsung Android phone or tablet, you can bring along your contacts, calendar appointments and texts, using a free app called Samsung Smart Switch Mobile, which can be downloaded from the Google Play store. Then you need to do the following:

1. Sign into iCloud on your iPhone or iPad, which can be done by going into **Settings** and scrolling down until you find **iCloud**.

2. In the iCloud settings page, press where it says Storage & Backup, then select to **Back Up Now**.

3. Now move back to your Samsung Android phone or tablet and open the **Smart Switch Mobile** app.

4. Agree to the terms and select to **Import from iCloud**. You will then need to sign in with your Apple ID.

5. You will then be given a list of the types of items to transfer. Once you've made your selections, press **Import**.

CONTACTS APP

This is where all of your newly imported numbers and email addresses can be found in alphabetical order. It's also the place where you access some of the main calling features.

Above: The Samsung Smart Switch app can be downloaded for free to import contacts from Apple.

How to Add a Contact

1. Press the + button; this will give you the option to **save the contact** to device, SIM card, Google account or Samsung account.

2. Type in the **name and phone number** in the respective fields by using the on-screen keyboard. You can also add an email address and assign a ringtone to the contact.

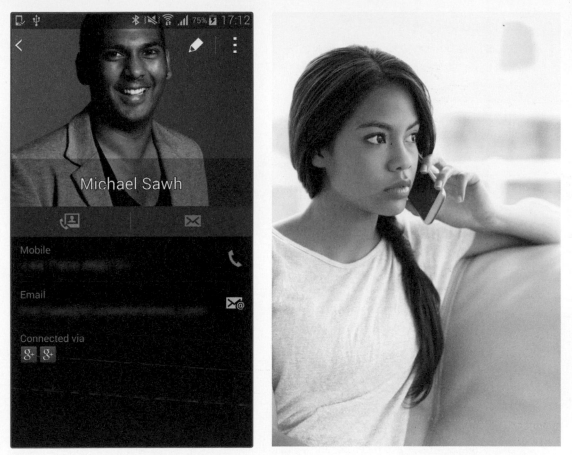

Step 4: Your new contact will now appear in the Contacts app.

3. In order to divide contacts into groups, such as family, friends, co-workers and emergency contacts, press **Groups**. Press the group you want to tick it, or press **Create** to make a new group.

4. Once you've finished entering contact details, press **Save**. The contact will now appear in the contacts app.

SPEED DIAL

Assigning contacts to speed dial will let you call them directly from the keypad. To set up speed dial:

1.   Click Settings and select **Speed dial**.

2.   Next to each number you will see **+ Add contact**. Press this and to bring up your contacts.

3.   **Scroll** down the list to find the contact and add it to a number on the keypad.

4.   To use speed dial, **press down** on the keypad number assigned to the contact.

CALL LOGS

This is where you can see, in chronological order, a recording of all the call activity, including calls made and received, and numbers dialed and rejected. Contacts can be contacted through the call log.

FAVOURITES

Here you can add favourite contacts for quick access. Press the **+** to add contacts from your contact list.

◻ ⧉	H+ ⣿ 38% ⬛ 15:38
< Speed dial	

◉	1~100	◉

1	◖◗	Voicemail
2	+	Add contact
3	+	Add contact
4	+	Add contact
5	+	Add contact
6	+	Add contact
7	+	Add contact
8	+	Add contact

Above: Speed dial will help you stay in touch with your closest contacts.

Hot Tip

You can use Google Voice search or Samsung S Voice (*see* page 104) to make calls without needing to go into the Contacts or keypad.

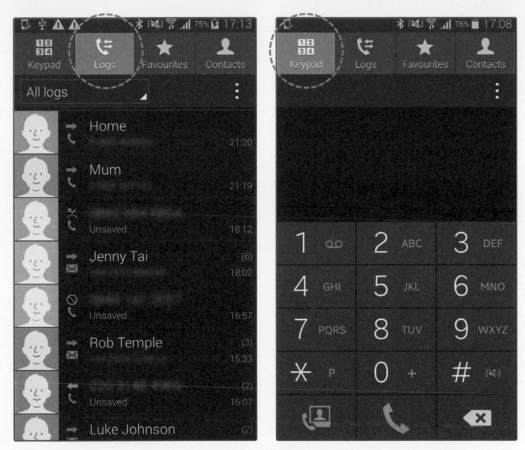

Above: You can contact people through the Call Logs section.

Step 1: To make a call, first open the dialing pad.

MAKING A CALL

One of the ways to make calls is to locate the Phone app icon and then do the following.

1. Open the **dialling pad**.

2. Type the number by pressing on the keys, then press the **green phone** icon to dial it.

3. If you've made a mistake when typing the number, the arrow with the cross on it will delete the numbers.

Alternatively, you can make a phone call by going to Contacts and scrolling down with a swipe of your finger to find the number you are looking for. You can also make a call from recently made or answered call by going to Logs and then scrolling down with a swipe. Press on Call details and press the green telephone icon to make the call.

ENDING A CALL

When you have finished a call, simply press End call and the phone will hang up and return to the home screen.

ANSWERING A CALL

There are a number of ways to deal with an incoming call.

○ Press or drag the **Accept Call** button to answer a call.

○ Drag a finger across the **Reject Call** icon to reject the call.

○ In order to move the call to speakerphone, answer it and then press the **Speaker** button.

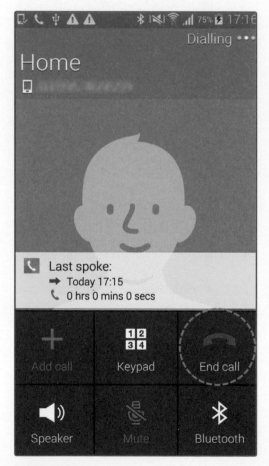

Above: Press End call to hang up.

SECURITY

When you are storing and accessing a great amount of private data, it's important to make sure that you take all the necessary precautions by applying settings that will help you to protect all that sensitive information. We are now going to have a look at the main security features.

FIND MY MOBILE

If your phone is stolen, you can make it easier to find by setting up Find My Mobile. This will help you to locate the device, lock it remotely so that someone else can't use It, and ring the phone to help identify its whereabouts.

Set up Find My Mobile

1. Go to **Settings**, select **Security** and turn on **Remote controls**.

2. Go to the **Find My Mobile** website (findmymobile.samsung.com/login.do), where you can sign in with your Samsung account and follow the instructions to create a Find My Mobile account.

VPN

If you are going to use your phone or tablet for work purposes, setting up a VPN (Virtual

Above: Find My Mobile can help you locate your phone.

Private Network) can help to protect against hackers accessing your private details and passwords when using public Wi-Fi hotspots.

Setting up a VPN

1. Got to **Settings**, select **More networks** and press **VPN**.

2. You may be asked to set a **screen unlock** PIN or password before proceeding, for which you can follow the instructions provided in the Lock Screen section (*see* page 37).

3. **Press +** to add VPNs. In the new window pop-up, type in a **name** for the VPN connection and select connection type.

4. Type in the **server address**, which will be provided by your service provider.

5. Click **Save** to store the settings.

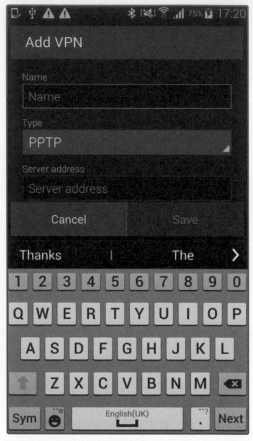

Step 4: Type in a name for the VPN connection.

6. Type in the **password and username** from your service provider. Click **Connect** and the new VPN connection will be completed.

FACTORY RESTORE

There might be times when the device has a few problems or you need to wipe the data to resell the phone. Performing a factory data reset will delete all files, including photos and video, and return the phone or tablet to the same state as when you first took it out of the box.

Before performing a factory restore, make sure that your personal files are backed up or saved to a computer.

Factory Restore in Settings

Go to Settings and select Backup and reset, then select Factory Data reset. The device will then take a few minutes to return to the original starting point before the setup process described in the Getting Started chapter.

Factory Restore with the Power and Volume Keys

Above: Make sure you back up data before performing a factory restore.

1. If you can't get into the Settings menu for whatever reason, with the device turned off, hold the **Volume up** button and the **on/off** button.

2. As the **Samsung logo** appears, let go of the on/off button but keep pressing the Volume up button.

3. You should now see the Android logo and a selection of options. Use the volume buttons to navigate to **Wipe Data/Factory Reset** and press the on/off button to confirm the action.

4. Use the volume button to select **Yes** and press the on/off button.

5. Navigate to the option again using the volume keys to select **Reboot System Now** and press the on/off button to confirm.

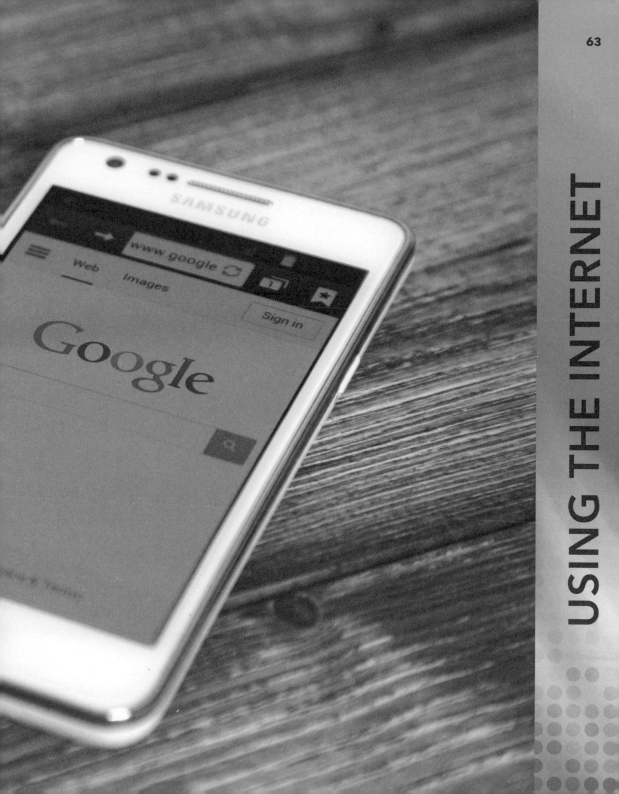

USING THE INTERNET

GETTING CONNECTED

In order to do all sorts of things, like browse the web, send emails or find your way around with maps, you first need to get connected to the internet, which can be done using a number of different methods.

WI-FI

One of the ways to connect to the internet when setting up a phone or tablet is to use a wireless connection – or Wi-Fi connection, as it's also known. If you are setting up the device for the first time and have already gone through the process described in the Getting Started chapter (*see page 16–17*), you should already be connected to the Wi-Fi or an internet connection. If you need to connect to a new Wi-Fi network, here's what you need to do.

Connect to a New Wi-Fi Network

1. Drag a finger down the top of the screen to open the **notification tray**. On older tablets, swipe up from the notification bar below and press the Settings cog icon.

2. Press the **Wi-Fi** button.

3. Make sure that the **Wi-Fi toggle** is turned on; it should be green at this point.

4. The phone or tablet will **scan** for all available networks and bring up a list.

5. Identify the new network to which you want to connect and select it. If it's an open Wi-Fi network then there will be no padlock and you should instantly be able to connect. You might also need to go into the web browser to sign in, as you would do for a Wi-Fi connection in a hotel room.

Above: The padlock indicates that the connection is secured by a password.

6. For the password protected networks, another screen will appear where you can type in the password. Once you are finished typing, press **Connect** and you should be ready to go.

MOBILE INTERNET

The other way to connect to the internet, when you are away from a Wi-Fi connection, is through a mobile internet connection. This works via the SIM, micro SIM or the smaller nano SIM card provided by your phone network provider and is dependent on the type of contract you have. Some Samsung tablets support mobile internet, as long they have a SIM card slot.

Types of Mobile Internet

The two most common types of mobile internet connection are 3G and 4G. The 'G' stands for generation, referring to third and fourth generation versions. These are the key differences.

- **3G**: This is the most common mobile internet connection and has the greatest coverage. If you mostly use your phone for voice calls, messages, checking in on Facebook and some browsing then this is the best option.

- **4G**: This offers the fastest mobile internet speeds and download speeds, which is useful if you like to download large videos on the move. 4G coverage in the UK is not yet widespread, so it won't be of benefit to everyone and, as with anything new, it does cost more to use.

Connecting to Mobile Internet

As long as the SIM or micro SIM card is secure inside the compartment behind the removable back of the phone or tablet, mobile internet will activate when it's available. That can entirely depend on your location, and coverage of different areas of the country and around the globe.

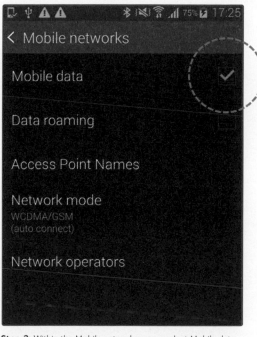

How to Connect to a Mobile Internet Network

1. Go to **Settings** and look for the icon or option called **Mobile networks**.

2. Press **Mobile networks** and then **Mobile data**. When there is a green tick alongside it, mobile data will be activated.

3. Samsung Android devices include the option to switch Mobile data on or off from the **Settings toggle** inside the notification tray.

4. Swipe down at the top of the screen (or from the bottom on older tablets) to bring up the **notification tray** and the Settings toggle.

5. Swipe right until you see the **Mobile data** button. Press this to fade out the icon and it will now be switched off. Press again to light it up and turn back on.

Step 2: Within the Mobile networks menu, select Mobile data.

Hot Tip

Use 4G coverage checkers available on network provider websites to see if you are in the best area to benefit from having 4G internet access.

Data Allowance

While there are many networks that offer unlimited mobile internet access, some will give you a specific data allowance per month. Although some networks will give you a warning via a text message to let you know when you are getting close to that amount, there are also other ways to keep an eye on your limit.

DATA USAGE

This feature (which works with Android 4.0 Ice Cream Sandwich or above) can help to monitor how much mobile internet data you use each month. It won't be the same way your service provider monitors data usage but it can give you a rough idea so you don't go over your mobile data limit. You can disable internet access when you are not on a Wi-Fi connection, for example.

Setting up Data Usage

1. Go to Settings and select the option called **Data usage**.

2. If Mobile data is turned on, the box beside it should have a green **tick**.

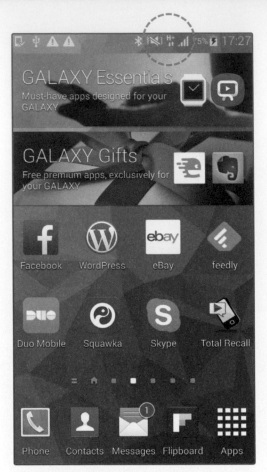

Above: A small H+, 3G or 4G icon should appear in the status indicator bar when you are connected.

Hot Tip

If you press Settings in Data usage, you can also choose to monitor data roaming, restrict background data and auto show Wi-Fi usage.

Step 3: Select Set mobile data limit.

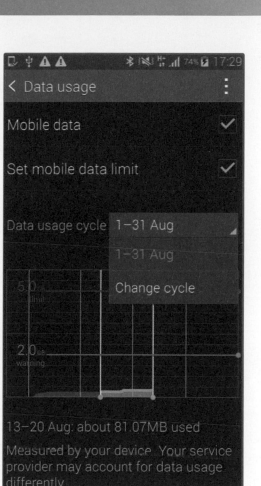

Step 4: Adjust Data Usage depending on the time you want to monitor.

3. Press **Set mobile data limit**, which will tell you that your mobile data connection will be disabled once the specified limit is reached.

4. In order to change the period monitored, press the small arrow in the box alongside **Data usage cycle**. Here you can customize when the measurement begins.

5. Underneath it is a **graph** with two movable bars that you can swipe inwards or outwards to see how much data has been used in a specific date range.

6. If you scroll down, you can also see **current apps** running and how much data they are currently consuming. This can help to give you an idea of the most data-heavy applications.

7. By pressing on the apps you will be able to see the amount of foreground and background **data** that they are using. The latter is used to quietly keep apps updated.

DATA ROAMING

Most phone networks will not account in your contract for using mobile internet when you go abroad, and accessing it can lead to big charges added to your monthly bill.

Turn Data Roaming On and Off

1. Go to **Settings** and select More Settings.

2. Press **Mobile networks**.

3. Press on the box alongside **Data roaming** and when it's ticked, data roaming will be turned on.

TETHERING AND MOBILE HOTSPOT

Tethering is a way of using the mobile internet connection and turning it into a Wi-Fi hotspot so that other internet-enabled devices, such as tablets or smartphones, can use it.

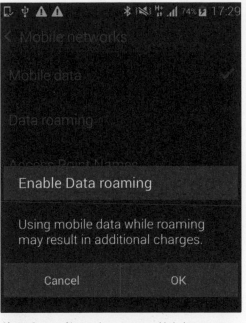

Above: Beware of having data roaming enabled when you go abroad.

Setting up a Mobile Hotspot

1. Go to **Settings**, select **Tethering and Mobile hotspots**, and choose to turn on the mobile hotspot by swiping the toggle to the right so that it turns green.

2. A notification will appear at the top of the screen to indicate that tethering or the mobile hotspot is **active**.

3. Press the icon showing three dots to choose which devices are allowed to **connect**. Press + to add other devices.

Above: Create a Wi-Fi connection for other devices to use.

4. You can also configure the hotspot by **naming it** something memorable and setting up a password.

5. You can choose when to **disable** mobile hotspot settings **automatically** if there are no connected devices. You can pick from between five and 60 minutes.

6. In order to connect from another device, turn on the Wi-Fi, select **AndroidAP** in the internet connection settings, type in the password and you should be connected.

7. Using a mobile hotspot will have an impact on **data usage** so think about when you are going to use it.

BROWSING

So now that you are connected to the internet, it's time to get to know the best way to browse the web.

USING THE BROWSER

In order to locate the internet browser, you need to look for the icon shaped like the Earth. It could already be present in the dock below the main home screen or found by searching all the apps via the app launcher.

● **Address bar**: This can be found at the top of the browser and it's where website URLs appear. When you press on the address bar, the on-screen keyboard will appear to let you type in an address.

● **Microphone**: At the end of the search bar is a microphone that, when pressed, activates Google Voice Search. This means that you can search for websites using your voice. Mention a website or query you are looking for and it will begin to search for it.

● **Arrows**: These will let you skip backwards and forwards between the current and previous web pages that you have visited.

● **Home**: Identified by the small house icon, pressing this will take you back to the browser homepage.

Above: Press the microphone icon to search the browser using your voice.

● **Save Page**: When you would like to save a web page, press this button; or Menu, then Save page on older models, and you can view all of the previously saved pages.

● **Quick Access**: When you first launch the browser, there will be a selection of websites listed that, when pressed, will jump directly to the site.

Hot Tip

In order to read web pages later when you no longer have an internet connection, press Save page (or Menu, save Page) and it will be stored on your smartphone or tablet.

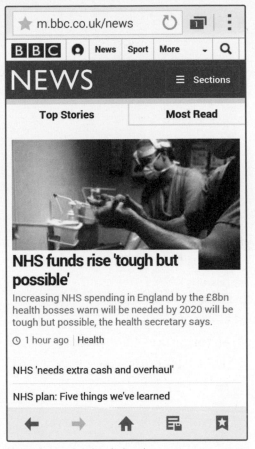

Above: Once you have launched a web page, new options appear above and below it.

- **Bookmark**: The icon with the little star will bookmark web pages for you. When on a page, press the icon and then press the **+** on the next screen to add it. Type in what you want to call it, press Done on the pop-up keyboard and then press Save.

WEB PAGE OPTIONS WHEN BROWSING

Once you have typed a URL into the address bar and launched a web page, you will find that you have some new options available to you.

- In the address bar, to the left of the website address, you will now see a **star**. Press this to **bookmark** the page.

- Also in the address bar, to the right of the web address, is a **circular arrow**. Press the arrow to **refresh** the page, to make sure that you are looking at the most recent version.

○ Further along the address bar you will see a **small square** with a number inside it. This indicates how many **web pages** you currently have open.

○ Press the icon to see all of the apps in the **Window manager**. You can swipe to close them or press a window to reopen the web page.

NEW WEB PAGE SETTINGS WHEN BROWSING

When you press the Settings icon, you will notice that you now have some new options:

○ **Share via**: Press this to share the web page. You will see a host of options, including email, Facebook, Google+ and Twitter. Press on the app you want to share it with and this will carry the link into the app, giving you space to write an additional message. Press Share to post.

○ **Add Shortcut to Home**: Press this to add the current web page to your browser home screen, thus adding it as one of the Quick Access websites.

Above: After pressing Share via, you will see there are several options for sharing a web page.

Above: Pressing Add Shortcut to Home will also add it as one of the Quick Access websites.

Above: With Find on page, you can locate words and phrases on the web page.

○ **Find on page**: When you press this, the address bar will be replaced by a search bar and the keyboard will appear. Now you can type to find a specific word or term on the page. When the word is identified, it will be highlighted on the page to help you locate it.

Above: View previously visited pages in the browser history.

BROWSING HISTORY

If you want to look back at the web pages that you have visited throughout the day, during the past few days or even further back, press the Bookmark icon to display a folder with a clock beside it. This is the browser History folder. If you want to clear the history, press the Settings button in the top right-hand corner and select Delete. Some older Samsung tablets will alternatively provide the option to Clear History, which will perform the same function.

MAPS

One of the most useful features you can find on smartphones and tablets is the ability to use GPS satellite signals – much like the sat navs you use in a car – to help you find your way around.

SETTING UP NAVIGATION SETTINGS

Before you launch the Maps app, you need to make sure that your device has the correct settings switched on.

1. Go to **Settings** and then **Location**.

2. You need to make sure that the **GPS location data** is turned on. Press the toggle at the top of the screen: when it's green, it's activated.

GOOGLE MAPS

Samsung uses the popular Google Maps app for navigation. This is found across all Android devices and is regularly updated, thus adding new features to help with your journey.

Above: Maps will give you the best route to your destination.

Setting up Google Maps

1. Launch the **Google Maps** app and agree to the terms of service and privacy policy.

2. Press **Accept** and **Continue**.

3. Google will request to **store your location**. This is not essential and you can say no if you prefer. However, opting in can help to generate more accurate directions and navigations.

Using Google Maps

○ The map should **pinpoint** exactly where you are.

○ Swipe two fingers outwards to **zoom in**.

○ Swipe two fingers inwards to **zoom out**.

○ Press the **radar button** and this will zoom into your precise current location.

○ Press **Search** to look for a place.

Google Maps Navigation

When you are struggling to read the map and you need some help to get to a location, you can use Google Maps Navigation.

1. In the Maps app, press the **arrow icon** inside the search bar at the top of the screen.

Hot Tip

Once you've picked a location, swipe up from the bottom of the screen and you will see an option to 'save map to use offline'. You will then be able to access it even when not connected to the internet.

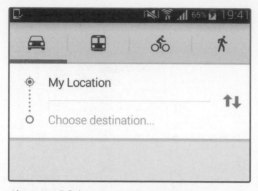

Above: Step 2: Pick your method of transport from the relevant icons to get accurate directions.

2. This will take you to a screen where, across the top, you can see **icons** for driving, public transport, cycling and walking navigation.

3. Press on the icon to select your **method of travel**.

4. Press **My Location** or **Starting Point** and you will be able to type in your current location. You can alternatively press the **My Location** tab with a small radar icon to let the device work out where you are.

5. Type in your destination in the **Choose destination** field.

6. Once you have finished, the app will return to the map and you will see a **red marker** identifying your destination and a **blue line** marking the route.

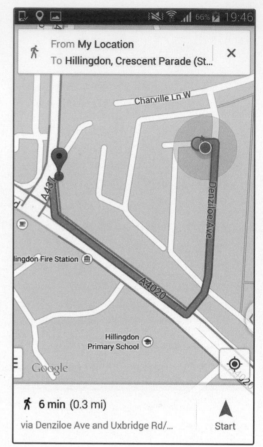

Step 6: The blue route will lead the way to your destination, as indicated by the red marker.

7. Below you'll see a calculation of how long it will take to get there.

8. Press the **Start** icon and the map will change and read out directions, just like a standard sat nav.

Google Maps Settings

Tucked away in the bottom left-hand corner of the Maps app, or from the Menu, you'll find additional settings that can assist you in your travels.

○ **Traffic**: This option will display the busiest and quietest roads for traffic by using colours. Green equals quiet, yellow means that roads are slightly busy and red indicates when roads are very busy.

○ **Satellite**: This changes the map to a view that uses more detailed satellite images so you can get a closer look at areas and places.

○ **Google Earth**: Once you have downloaded the Google Earth app from the Google Play Store, you can look at places across the world via 3-D imagery so you can explore with virtual tours.

Above: You can view maps using satellite imagery.

Hot Tip

To look back at previous journeys and navigations, go to the Maps tab, select Settings and press Map history.

EMAIL

You can check your emails wherever you are, with your Samsung mobile device. You can already use the Gmail account you acquired when setting up your Android device, but you can also use other email accounts.

SETTING UP AN EMAIL ACCOUNT

1. Go to the **Email** app and type in the email address you want to access, along with the password you use to log into the account.

2. Press **Next**. The device will display a message, saying that it is **Checking for incoming server settings**. If successful, it will present you with a series of options:

○ **Dropdown menu**: Here you can view your inbox, set up priority senders, see messages sent and view all folders created.

○ **Refresh**: This updates the account to make sure you have the most up-to-date version.

○ **Search**: This lets you search your emails.

○ **Folders**: Any folders you have created will appear here; press + to add new folders.

Step 1: Type in the email address and password for the account you want to access.

SENDING AN EMAIL

1. Open the **Email** app and press the pen on paper icon.

2. In the **To** section, type in the recipient. Press the down arrow to copy in others.

3. Type in the **Subject field**, then write your message in the blank field.

4. If you want to send an **attachment**, press the paperclip. This will open the apps and programs from which you can attach files, such as images, audio files or even a phone contact.

5. Press the **X** if you want to cancel the email. Press the **disk icon** to save it.

6. To send, press the icon at the top of the screen with the **envelope and arrow**.

Step 2: Type in the recipient's email address.

Replying to an Email

Press the small icon with an arrow pointing backwards. If it's an email with multiple recipients, press the icon with two arrows. Now you will be able to compose the message in the field below. Press the email icon to send the message.

Forwarding an Email

If you simply want to pass on the details of a received email without altering the information, press the icon with a straight arrow. Then type in the recipients and tap the email icon to send.

Alarm	AllShare Pl...	Calculator	Camera
Dropbox	Email	G+ Photos	Gallery
Google+	Group Play	Help	Internet
aper Artist	Phone	Play Store	Polaris Offi...
amsung	Settings	Smart Re	Talk

tON

Contacts

Crayon ph...

Downloads

e Hub

Gmail

Google

Google Set...

ps

Messaging

Music Play...

My Files

ouch

S Note

S Planner

S Voice

:ditor

Video Player

Voice Sear

World Clock

APPS

NEW APPS

One of the reasons why smartphones and tablets are so popular is largely thanks to the apps that you can download and use on them. These small programs, which can live on the home screen and tucked away in the app drawer, can unlock new features and make greater use of your device's key features.

Hot Tip

If you are not happy with an app that you have purchased, you can get a refund within the first 2 hours of owning it.

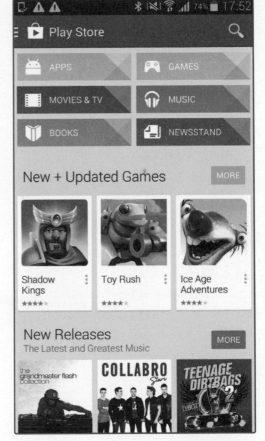

Above: Google Play is where you can download apps and much more.

GOOGLE PLAY STORE

Just like the iTunes Store for the iPhone and the iPad, Google Play is a shop where you can download free and paid for apps directly to your smartphone or tablet. You can also download books, music, games, magazines and newspapers.

Create a Google Play Account

To set one up you need to add a Google account. If you haven't already done it in the initial setup process, this is how to do it.

1. Go to **Settings** and click on **Accounts**.

2. Press **+ Add account** and select **Google**. You will when be asked to go through the same setup that is explained in the Getting Started chapter (*see* pages 18–23).

3. In order to access **Google Play**, press on the Apps icon or look for the shopping bag icon already on the main home screen.

Navigating the Google Play Store

- Once inside the Google Play Store, you will see **categories** for apps, games, movies and TV, music, books and newsstand. Each of these sections can be explored to find apps.

- If you swipe down the main Google Play screen, you will see app and content **recommendations** which might also interest you.

- At the top of the screen is the magnifying glass or **search icon** to browse for specific apps.

DOWNLOADING AN APP

Here we will show you how to download an app. The same principle applies when downloading games and other content from the Google Play Store.

1. Press on **Apps**.

2. Swipe left and right to see the apps presented in a series of **categories**.

3. Once you have found an app that you want, **press** on it.

4. Next you'll see a description of the app, and there will be a green box with the words **Free** or a price contained inside.

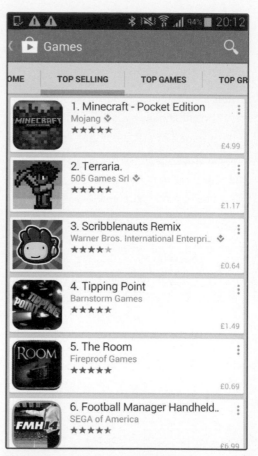

Above: You can search for new and top-selling apps.

5. When you press on a paid app, you'll see the type of **Access** that it requires before you make the purchase.

6. You can see these requests in more detail by pressing the small arrows beside each of the individual access requests. Once you are happy, hit **Accept** and the app will start downloading.

7. If you are downloading a **free** app, you will be prompted to install straight away. If it's a **paid** app and you have already registered a credit card, it will proceed to download.

8. If you haven't registered a **credit card**, you can do so at this point, and your details will be saved for future purchases (*see* page 25).

9. The app will **install** and be ready to use.

10. You will have to **wait** until one download has finished before you can download another app.

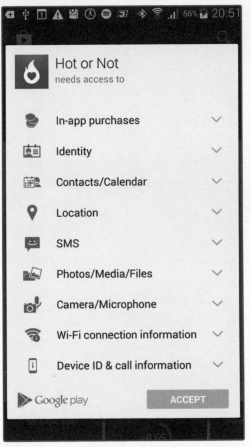

Step 5: You can view access requests before deciding whether to download.

FIND THE DOWNLOADED APP

If the app has installed correctly, it should appear in the app drawer ready to be used. Look for the Apps icon and swipe through to scroll and identify the app.

Above: Register a credit card to enable you to purchase apps.

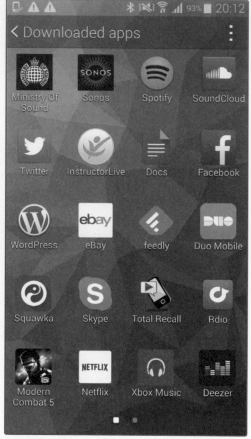

Above: You can choose to view only downloaded apps for example, to find the one you want to delete.

HOW TO DELETE APPS

If there is an app that you no longer want or you need to free up some space, go into **Settings** and look for the **Application manager**. This is where you can view all the apps that exist on your device. You can choose to view by: Downloaded; the ones installed on the SD card; those currently running; or simply all the applications installed.

Go to the relevant section and swipe down to search for the app that you want to delete. Once located, press on it and select the option to **Uninstall**. Select to Uninstall on the next window and the app will be removed from the device.

GOOGLE APPS

Every Android phone or tablet comes with a set of apps designed by Google. They should already be installed and can range from making notes to finding the best way to get to work.

GOOGLE NOW

Google Now (available on devices with Android 4.1 Jelly Bean and above) is an intelligent virtual assistant that can deliver useful information without the user needing to search for it. Before you use it, there are a number of settings that you need to activate in order for it to work.

SETTING UP GOOGLE NOW

1. In order to launch **Google Now**, hold down the **Home** button and press **Next**.

2. In order to get the best use of Google Now, you'll need to agree for Google to use and **store your location** for features such as traffic alerts and directions.

3. You then need to decide whether to use synced calendars, Gmail, Chrome and

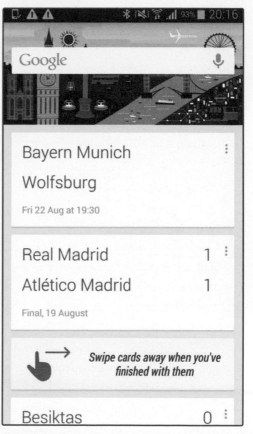

Above: Google Now is an application that learns about the information you need.

Google data so that Google Now reminders can work properly. If you agree, press the button that says **Yes**, **I'm in**.

4. If you have multiple accounts, you will be asked to **choose one** of them. Once decided, click the account.

5. This will open the Google Now interface. You can launch the Google Now application by pressing down on the **Home button**.

Getting to Know Google Now

○ At the top of the app you will see the Google Voice Search bar. Press the **microphone** to begin a voice search or press the search bar to type a query.

○ Underneath that you will find **cards** based on search data. You can swipe right on cards when you have finished with them.

Above: Google Now uses voice to search the internet.

○ Each card has a **settings app**, which will often ask whether you are interested in the topic. This will help to make sure that information is better tailored to your interests in the future.

○ In order to improve suggestions, you can enable **Location reporting**. This is useful for traffic alerts.

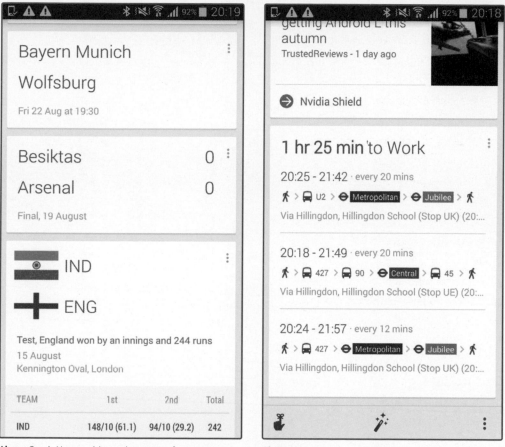

Above: Google Now can deliver real-time scores for sporting events.

Above: Google Now can calculate routes to work.

- Select **High accuracy** or **Battery-saving location mode** to determine location and deliver localized weather and commuting traffic.

Customizing Google Now

- The **little wand** lets you customize Google Now. Click on the different categories and set what you are interested in; this covers Sports, Stocks, Place and Everything Else.

○ In the **Everything Else** section, you can specify how you usually get around, how you commute and whether you are interested in weather updates.

○ Press the **three-dotted icon** to jump into the same settings that have been described previously (see page 41).

GOOGLE DRIVE

Cloud storage is becoming a major part of how smartphones and tablets can store content, including photos, documents and videos, thus giving you access whenever you are online.

Setting up Google Drive

1. If the Google Drive app is not installed on your device, go to the Google Play Store to download it for **free**.

2. You will need to **log in** using your Google account.

3. Once you are signed in, you will be able to **upload** content, **create** documents and spreadsheets, and **scan** images using the built-in camera in your device.

Above: Google Drive uses cloud storage to save documents and files.

Hot Tip

Use the + or @ sign to mention someone in a Google+ post.

Using Google Drive

- To create a document, press **+ Create** and choose whether to make a new folder, document or spreadsheet.

- Press **Upload** and you will be able to search through files on your device. Find the one you want and press to upload it.

- When you sign into Google Drive on a computer or another device, you will still have **access** to all of the content that you have uploaded.

GOOGLE+

Google+ is a social networking site where you can share posts and videos and also back up content such as photos taken on your device.

Creating a Google+ Account

1. The first thing you need is a **Google account**. You should have one of those, as it's required to access other features, such as Google Play.

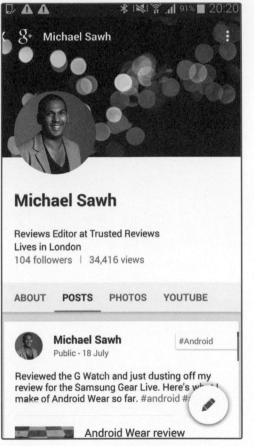

Above: Google+ is a social networking service with a few other tricks.

2. You will be asked if you want to keep you address book up to date and **unify** Google+ connections with phone or tablet contacts. Tick or untick the box depending on preference.

3. Press **Done**.

Google+ Features

Now that you are signed up, it's time to get familiar with the key aspects of Google+. It is like a mixture of Facebook, Twitter, Instagram and a whole host of other sites.

- **Profile page**: Located by the drop-down menu in the top left-hand corner, this is the page where you can fill in your bio, write posts, add photos and pull in video content from your YouTube channel, if you have one set up.

- **People**: Here you will see suggestions of people who you can add to your Google+ connections by pressing the Add button beside them.

- **Communities**: This is where you can join groups and have conversations with other people who share similar interests. Updates from those new communities will filter into your Google+ news stream.

- **Photos**: If you opt to back up your camera, any of the photos you take will be uploaded here so that you will always have a copy. Photos can be uploaded over Wi-Fi or a mobile network.

- **Circles**: When you add people as connections, you can put them in groups or Circles. These can be Friends, Family or people you are following.

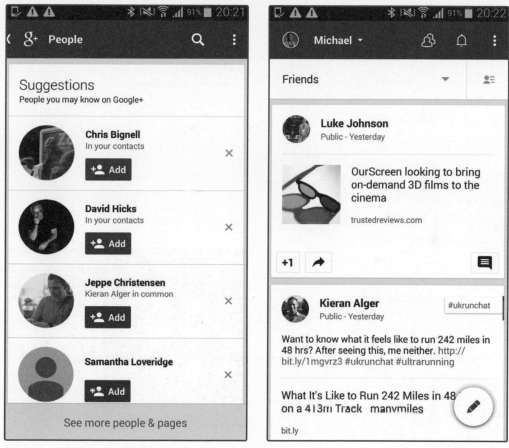

Above: Create a profile and post from your Google+ page.

Above: Create circles for friends, families and work colleagues.

GOOGLE HANGOUTS

This is an instant messaging service that also lets you make video calls with multiple Google users at the same time. Think of it as a bit like Facetime for iPhone or Skype. You can connect with people in your Google+ circles.

Using Google Hangouts

1. Look for the icon with the green **speech bubble** and **speech marks**, and you have found Hangouts.

2. When you first launch it, you will be asked if you want to **Turn on SMS**. This means that you will be able to see all your text messages in one conversation, along with conversations made inside Hangouts.

3. What you will then see is a list of your phone **contacts** and people who want to hang out with you.

4. Swipe left to reveal a drop-down menu where **recent** Hangouts instant message **conversations** and **invites** are recorded.

Make a Call in Google Hangouts

1. Find your **contact** and select it.

2. You will see a **video camera icon** in the top corner. Press to initiate a video call.

3. If you want to have an instant message conversation, start typing in the field where it says **Send Hangouts message**. The smiley face lets you add emoticons and the paperclip lets you attach files.

Step 3: Press the smiley face to add emoticons.

Hot Tip

You can share Google Docs in real time during a Hangouts video call so that all participants can collaborate on the one document.

Step 2: Touch Anyone Else to add more contacts.

Make a Group Video Call in Google Hangouts

1. In your Hangouts app, swipe right on the screen, then press the + icon.

2. Begin typing the names of the people with whom you want to have a conversation, then touch **Anyone Else?** to add more contacts and press **OK**.

3. When you have finished, hit the **video camera icon**.

GOOGLE PLAY APPS

Google Play apps are a selection of apps available on all Samsung tablets and smartphones. They are there to help you make the most of the content that you can download and purchase from the Google Play Store, whether that's video, books, music or even newspapers.

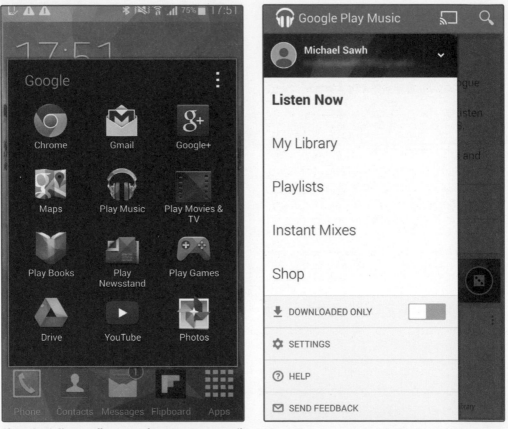

Above: Google Play apps offer a variety of ways to entertain yourself.

Above: Store your music in the cloud so you can listen anywhere.

PLAY GAMES

If you like playing games, Play Games is all about making the experience more sociable. Here you can compete with friends, track achievements and pick up wherever you left off, on another Google smartphone or tablet.

PLAY NEWSSTAND

This brings you all your favourite news and magazines together in a single app. It pulls in stories from websites.

PLAY BOOKS

If you want to read books, Play Books is the place to do it. You can browse and shop for books, some of which are free, or check out recommendations.

Above: Catch up on the latest news in Newsstand.

PLAY MOVIES & TV

This is the place for all of your film and TV video purchases. Buy them in the Google Play store and they will appear in this app to watch.

PLAY MUSIC

This is the Google music app where you can listen to all your music both offline and online. It's also a music streaming subscription service where you can pay a monthly fee and get access to a catalogue of music. Additionally, you can store your own songs in Google's Play Music cloud locker.

SAMSUNG APPS

Along with the Google Play apps, Samsung also includes a suite of its own apps. They can vary from device to device but these are the core applications that you should expect to see.

MY GALAXY APP

This is a Samsung-only app where you can find out how to get the most out of your Samsung Galaxy smartphone and the benefits of being a Samsung customer. Here you can get exclusive offers from film, music and entertainment content to tickets for events.

GALAXY APPS

Like the Google Play Store, Samsung has its own app store where you can get many of the same Android apps. Additionally, it will grant you free access to apps for which you would normally have to pay. It will also pick apps that are best optimized for Samsung devices.

S VOICE

S Voice is available on Android 4.1 Jelly Bean upwards. It's the voice recognition software that lets you perform tasks.

Above: Samsung has a suite of its own apps, available through the Galaxy app store.

Setting up S Voice

- Touch the S Voice icon in the App drawer. You will need to agree to the disclaimer.

- S Voice is activated when you tap the microphone or say, 'Hi Galaxy'.

- You can ask for today's weather, for example, and your question will be answered.

- It can also open apps, make calls, write texts, look up contacts, schedule events and play music, among other things.

S HEALTH

This is available on Android 4.4 KitKat upwards. You can activate S Health by double-tapping on the home button. S Health is an application that can help to manage your well-being, set fitness goals, check progress and keep track of your overall health.

CHATON

ChatON is available on Android 4.1 Jelly Bean upwards. It's Samsung's instant messaging service which you can only use to talk to other Samsung users.

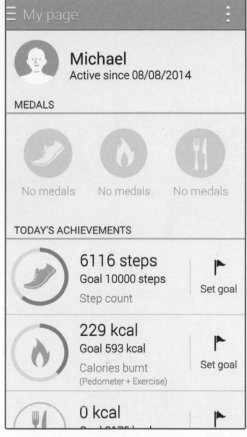

Above: S Health is an app to help you keep fit and stay healthy.

Hot Tip

You can also download apps and content from the web version of the Google Play Store (play.google.com/store).

PHOTOS, VIDEOS & MUSIC

PHOTOS

Smartphones and tablets can do so much more than just making calls and browsing the internet. You will no longer need to carry a camera around, thanks to your device's ability to take photos.

CAMERA APP

This is the place where you can take pictures and record video. Camera menus and options will vary on different devices but there are some core features that you should be able to use even with older models.

Using the Camera App

Look for the camera-shaped icon and press to launch. You'll find a series of different buttons around the screen; these are the important ones you need to know about.

- **Camera Button**: The circular button with the camera icon that, when pressed, takes the photo.

- **Record Button**: The video camera icon that, when pressed, will begin to make a video recording.

Below: Familiarise yourself with the main buttons in the camera app.

- **Camera Swap**: The button with a camera and arrows, which can switch between the front camera and the rear camera.

- **Settings**: The small cog opens up a host of other options and modes that you can apply to photos and video.

Camera Settings

The camera app caters for both beginners and more experienced photographers. These are some of the key camera features that you can expect to see.

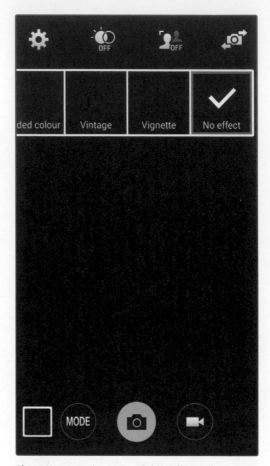

- **Flash**: Usually found on Samsung Android phones and tablets, turning the flash on can help you to take better pictures in low-light environments.

- **Picture size**: You can take photos in different levels of quality. This is measured by megapixels. The more megapixels, the larger the file size and better the quality. Pick a smaller picture size if you want to share something quickly on Facebook or via email.

- **Effects**: The magic wand icon can add a number of different filters to change the look of photos. When you open the Effects, you can view the options by swiping across with a finger to scroll.

Above: You can apply a variety of photo effects before taking pictures.

- **Timer**: This feature will give you time to get into the photo. PressTimer and select the duration of the countdown. When you next press the camera button, the remaining seconds will be displayed before it's ready to capture the image.

Above: You can focus in on objects by pressing on the screen.

How to Take a Photo

Now that you are familiar with the main camera settings, let's look at the quickest and easiest way to take a photo.

> # Hot Tip
>
> **Auto backup saves all your existing and new photos and videos to your private Google Photos account so that you will never lose them.**

1. Launch the **Camera** app.

2. Point and **aim** the screen at the object, person or scene you want to take a picture of.

3. Press on the screen to **focus** on a particular point in the scene.

4. You can use two fingers to pinch and **zoom** to move closer to objects.

5. Press the **Camera** button, and the photo is taken and saved to the device.

How to Take a 'Selfie'

If your smartphone or tablet includes a front-facing camera, you should be able to identify the camera sensor above the screen.

- ○ Inside the Camera app, press the **camera swap** button and the camera will now be facing you.

- ○ Press the **camera button** and the image is captured.

VIEWING PHOTOS

Now that your photos have been taken, there are a number of ways in which you can look back at them.

Above: Taking selfies are easy with the front-facing camera.

Viewing Photos in the Camera App

In the Camera app, look for the icon displaying a thumbnail image of the most recently taken photo. Press on the image and you will be taken straight into the Gallery app.

How to Delete a Photo

1. Press the thumbnail image in the bottom corner of the **Camera** app to bring up the stream of photos.

2. Swipe through the images to find the one you want to delete then press the dustbin icon. A message saying that **1 item will be deleted** will appear. Press **OK** to delete the photo.

3. You can also delete images from the **Gallery** app.

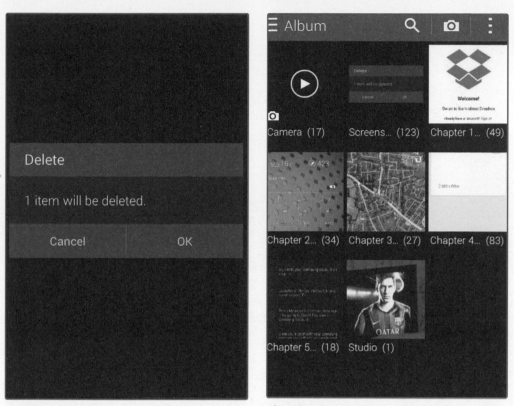

Step 2: Press OK to confirm you want to delete the photo.

Above: Press the three lines in the top corner to choose whether to view photos in albums or in chronological order.

GALLERY APP

This is the place dedicated to looking back at photos and videos taken on your phone or tablet. It can also provide access to saved images from the web, apps, screenshots and edited images.

Using the Gallery App

- You can choose to review content by the date they were taken or by albums. Press the three lines in the corner to launch the drop-down menu and select **Time** or **Album**.

- In order to view photos in a slideshow, press Settings and select **Slideshow**.

- You can move to the Camera app to take photos by pressing the **camera icon** at the top of the screen.

Sharing Photos

1. Open a photo from the **Gallery** app.

2. Press the **Share** button and choose the app that you want to use to share your photo.

3. Once you have chosen, the image will be pulled through and you can add a **caption** or **post** it straight away.

Edit Photos

○ **Select** a photo and press the icon with the small pen, or on older models press Menu.

○ The **Crop** button will let you cut out parts of the image that you don't want.

○ The **Rotate** button will change which way up the image is.

○ If your device is running on Android 4.1 Jellybean or later you can also adjust the **tone**, add **effects**, and much more. Press the back and forward arrows to undo and redo changes.

○ Press the computer disk to **save** the edited image.

Above: You can edit images after they have been taken, such as cropping them.

Hot Tip

On newer Samsung Android devices you can turn on Voice Commands in the camera app. When you call out cheese it'll snap the photo hands-free.

VIDEOS

As well as taking photos, you can also use your smartphone or tablet like a video recorder. Filming is done from within the Camera app.

HOW TO TAKE A VIDEO

1. Open the **Camera** app.

2. Press on the **Record** button, which should be above the camera button.

3. The **red light** will appear on the screen to indicate that the recording has begun.

4. You can press the **Pause** or **Stop** button when you need to halt the recording.

5. Pinch the screen with two fingers to **zoom** into objects.

HOW TO VIEW VIDEOS

Recorded videos can be found in the Gallery app and are identified by a large play icon. Press on the thumbnail to open up the video and watch it in full screen.

Above: You can shoot video from the Camera app.

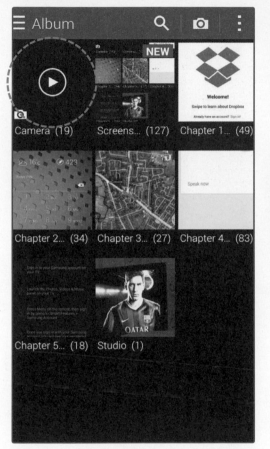

Above: Look for the Play sign to locate videos in the Gallery app.

TRIM VIDEOS

You can adjust the length, or remove pieces of video that you don't want, by using the video trimming feature.

How to Trim a Video

1. Select the video in the Gallery app, and press the **scissors** icon.

2. The next screen will display a **timeline**, showing the video frame by frame.

3. The two icons at the end of the timeline can be moved inwards and outwards to **cut** and trim the video.

4. When you've finished editing, press **Done**. Pick a name for the video and press **OK**.

SHARING VIDEOS

Sharing videos is done in a similar way to sharing pictures. When you select the video in the Gallery app, press the Share button and choose the place where you want to share it.

VIDEO APP

As well as creating videos, the Samsung Video app is another place where you can view them saved on your smartphone or tablet. You can also connect other devices, such as Samsung TVs, tablets and a PC, to share and view video right on your device.

Above: You can share videos through a range of apps and services.

How to Connect the Video App

○ In order to connect to a **PC**, you need to sign up to Samsung Link. This can be done via the Samsung website (http://link.samsung.com/).

○ For other **Samsung devices**, download the Samsung Link app from the Galaxy app store.

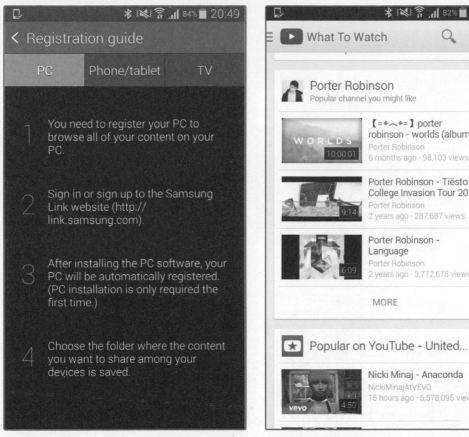

Above: You can share video from computers and TVs over Wi-Fi.   **Above:** The YouTube app comes preinstalled on all devices.

● **Samsung TVs** are also compatible, and you will need to sign into the Samsung account on the TV to create the connection.

YOUTUBE

The video sharing website comes pre-installed on Samsung Android phones and tablets. It gives you all of the same features, including sharing videos over email and via Google+, among other places.

MUSIC

You can use your tablet or smartphone like an MP3 player to listen to music. Samsung's Music app comes pre-installed and here's how to use it.

USING THE MUSIC APP

- When you open the **Music app**, sections are broken into Playlists, Tracks, Albums, Artists and Folders.

- The magnifying glass at the top of the screen will help you to **search** for specific music content using the on-screen keyboard.

- Like the Video app, you can create a connection with PCs, TVs and other tablets or smartphones which will allow you to **share** and **play** content **wirelessly**.

How to Play Music

When you find a track or album you want to listen to, press on the play icon on top of it to start playing. This will bring up the controller, where you can jump to different points of the song, as well as skipping backwards and forwards through tracks.

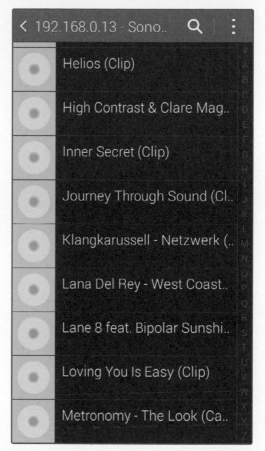

Above: Use the letters down the side to navigate through the list of tracks, albums or artists.

HOW TO TRANSFER MUSIC FROM A PC

If you have music stored on your computer which you want to store on your tablet or smartphone, you'll need to use the micro USB charging cable provided with your device to connect to a PC. Then you need to take the following steps.

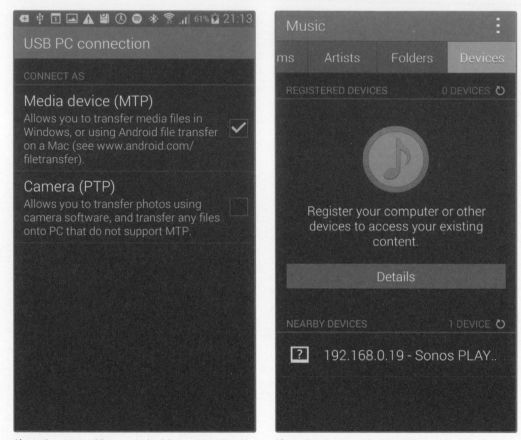

Above: Connect your PC to your Android device with a USB cable.　　**Above:** Download music from your PC to your Samsung device.

1.   When the device is connected to a PC, a window will appear called **Autoplay**.

2.   Select the option to **Open device** to view files. This will let you see all the files stored on the phone or tablet in folders similar to the ones you find on your PC.

3.   Once you have found the music that you want to transfer, you can drag and drop the files into the **Music folder** on your Samsung phone or tablet.

4. Safely remove the phone connected to the PC and when you go into the Music app, you should find the **new music** populated inside the app.

HOW TO TRANSFER MUSIC FROM A MAC

Transferring music from a Mac works slightly differently but should still be relatively straightforward if you stick to these simple steps.

1. On your **Mac**, download software called Android File Transfer from android.com/filetransfer/.

2. Once that is installed, connect the phone or tablet to the Mac using the supplied **micro USB to USB** cable.

Android File Transfer

For Mac users only. You don't need extra software to connect your Android device to a Windows computer.

Android File Transfer is an application for Macintosh computers (running Mac OS X 10.5 or later) you can use to view and transfer files between your Mac and an Android device (running Android 3.0 or later).

Download Now »

By downloading, you agree to our Terms of Service and Privacy Policy

Download and Install

- **Step 1:** Click Download Now above.
- **Step 2:** When the download completes, double-click androidfiletransfer.dmg.
- **Step 3:** In the Installer window, drag Android File Transfer to Applications.

Use Android File Transfer

- Use the USB cable that came with your Android device to connect it to your Mac.
- Double-click Android File Transfer to open it the first time (subsequently, it opens automatically).
- Browse the files and folders on your Android device, add folders, copy files up to 4GB to or from your Mac, delete files, and more.
- Choose Help > Android File Transfer Help to learn more.

Site Terms of Service | Privacy Policy | Brand Guidelines | Jobs

---

Above: To Import iTunes music from your Mac, first download Android File Transfer.

3. You should now see a small **notification** icon at the top of the screen or at the bottom that looks like an arrow with arms.

4. When you swipe down from the top of the screen (or up from the bottom of the screen on older tablets), you will now be able to see a **Connected as a media device** notification. Tap this and make sure you tick the box beside the option for **Media device (MTP)**.

5. Go to the **folder** on your Mac where the music you want to transfer is kept.

6. Drag and drop the files into the **Music folder** on the device.

7. Once the device is safely **disconnected**, open the Music app and music should now appear ready for playback.

Above: Use Bluetooth to connect to wireless headphones and speakers.

CONNECTIVITY

If you want to use wireless headphones or speakers and even send images to your TV, there are a number of ways for you to do so without using an internet connection.

Bluetooth

Bluetooth can be used to connect wirelessly to devices such as wireless headphones and speakers. In order to turn on Bluetooth, go to Settings then Bluetooth. Press the toggle and Scan to see available Bluetooth devices. When you see one that you recognize and it's in close proximity, press on it to pair.

Android Beam

Using NFC or Near Field Communication, Android Beam is similar to Bluetooth and is a way to wirelessly connect two devices to exchange data, such as pictures and documents. It works with Android 4.0 Ice Cream Sandwich or above.

In order to turn on NFC, go to Settings, press on NFC and swipe the toggle to activate. Now you will be able to share content over NFC by simply holding another phone or tablet with NFC turned on against the back of another Samsung Android phone or tablet with NFC enabled.

S Beam

S Beam works similarly to Android Beam but it uses something called Wi-Fi Direct to transfer data. Unique to Samsung devices, it can transfer data quickly and will only work between Samsung devices.

To turn it on, go to Settings, then Connections, then S Beam and toggle the slider.

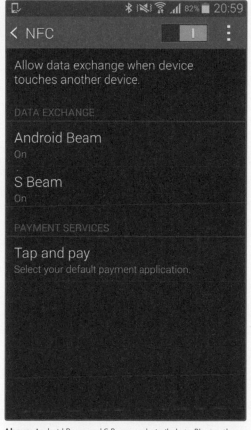

Above: Android Beam and S Beam work similarly to Bluetooth.

Hot Tip

In order to upload your own music, use the Google Music desktop manager from a PC or Mac. You can download it for free from the Google Play website.

USEFUL WEBSITES & FURTHER READING

WEBSITES

www.androidcentral.com
The website with everything from forums to 'how to' guides, as well as the latest news.

www.android-developers.blogspot.co.uk
A blog dealing with all things Android.

www.androidforum.com
A forum for Android users and enthusiasts regarding everything Android.

www.androidtablets.net
An informational forum about Android tablets.

www.beginandroid.com
A website which gives easy access to explanations for Android users.

www.developer.android.com
Latest apps and design news, as well as a guide on how to make apps.

www.everythingandroid.org
A website for questions, as well as shopping for Android.

www.networkworld.com/blog/android-angle/
A weekly updated blog which discusses Android development and technological news in general.

www.officialandroidblog.blogspot.co.uk
News and notes from the Android team.

www.techrepublic.com
A website containing data on an array of smartphones, including Android.

FURTHER READING

Annuzzi, Joseph Jr. *Introduction to Android Application Development: Android Essentials*, Addison-Wesley Professional, 2013

Clare, Andrew, *The Rough Guide to Android Phones and Tablets*, Rough Guides, 2012

Drake, Joshua J., *Android Hacker's Handbook,* Wiley, 2014

Elenkov, Nikolay, *Android Security Internals: An In-Dept Guide to Android's Security Architecture*, No Starch Press, 2014

Gookin, Dan, *Android for Dummies*, For Dummies, 2014

Hart-Davis, Guy, *Teach Yourself Visually Android Phones and Tablets*, Visual, 2013

Hellman, Erik, *Android Programming: Pushing the Limits*, Wiley, 2013

Hetch, Scott L., *Android from A to D*, CreateSpace Independent Publishing Platform, 2014

Murphy, Mark L., *Android Programming Tutorials*, CommonsWare LLC, 2010

Philips, Bill, *Android Programming: The Big Nerd Ranch Guide*, Big Nerd Ranch Guides, 2013

Talbot, James, *Learning Android Application Programming: A Hands-On Guide to Building Android Applications*, Addison-Wesley Professionals, 2014

INDEX